ELIZABETH

DEALING WITH DISAPPOINTMENT

A Bible study based on the teaching of

NANCY DEMOSS WOLGEMUTH

Elizabeth's story

AS FOUND IN LUKE 1

DEDICATION TO THEOPHILUS

[1] Inasmuch as many have undertaken to compile a narrative of the things that have been accomplished among us, [2] just as those who from the beginning were eyewitnesses and ministers of the word have delivered them to us, [3] it seemed good to me also, having followed all things closely for some time past, to write an orderly account for you, most excellent Theophilus, [4] that you may have certainty concerning the things you have been taught.

BIRTH OF JOHN THE BAPTIST FORETOLD

[5] In the days of Herod, king of Judea, there was a priest named Zechariah, of the division of Abijah. And he had a wife from the daughters of Aaron, and her name was Elizabeth. [6] And they were both righteous before God, walking blamelessly in all the commandments and statutes of the Lord. [7] But they had no child, because Elizabeth was barren, and both were advanced in years.

[8] Now while he was serving as priest before God when his division was on duty, [9] according to the custom of the priesthood, he was chosen by lot to enter the temple of the Lord and burn incense. [10] And the whole multitude of the people were praying outside at the hour of incense. [11] And there appeared to him an angel of the Lord standing on the right side of the altar of incense. [12] And Zechariah was troubled when he saw him, and fear fell upon him. [13] But the angel said to him, "Do not be afraid, Zechariah, for your prayer has been heard, and your wife Elizabeth will bear you a son, and you shall call his name John. [14] And you will have joy and gladness, and many will rejoice at his birth, [15] for he will be great before the Lord. And he must not drink wine or strong drink, and he will be filled with the Holy Spirit, even from his mother's

womb. [16] And he will turn many of the children of Israel to the Lord their God, [17] and he will go before him in the spirit and power of Elijah, to turn the hearts of the fathers to the children, and the disobedient to the wisdom of the just, to make ready for the Lord a people prepared."

[18] And Zechariah said to the angel, "How shall I know this? For I am an old man, and my wife is advanced in years." [19] And the angel answered him, "I am Gabriel. I stand in the presence of God, and I was sent to speak to you and to bring you this good news. [20] And behold, you will be silent and unable to speak until the day that these things take place, because you did not believe my words, which will be fulfilled in their time." [21] And the people were waiting for Zechariah, and they were wondering at his delay in the temple. [22] And when he came out, he was unable to speak to them, and they realized that he had seen a vision in the temple. And he kept making signs to them and remained mute. [23] And when his time of service was ended, he went to his home.

[24] After these days his wife Elizabeth conceived, and for five months she kept herself hidden, saying, [25] "Thus the Lord has done for me in the days when he looked on me, to take away my reproach among people."

BIRTH OF JESUS FORETOLD

[26] In the sixth month the angel Gabriel was sent from God to a city of Galilee named Nazareth, [27] to a virgin betrothed to a man whose name was Joseph, of the house of David. And the virgin's name was Mary. [28] And he came to her and said, "Greetings, O favored one, the Lord is with you!" [29] But she was greatly troubled at the saying, and tried to discern what sort of greeting this might be. [30] And the angel said to her, "Do not be afraid, Mary, for you have found favor with God. [31] And behold, you will conceive in your womb and bear a son, and you shall call his name Jesus. [32] He will be great and will be called the Son of the Most High. And the Lord God will give to him the throne of his father David, [33] and he will reign over the house of Jacob forever, and of his kingdom there will be no end."

[34] And Mary said to the angel, "How will this be, since I am a virgin?"

[35] And the angel answered her, "The Holy Spirit will come upon you, and the power of the Most High will overshadow you; therefore the child to be born will be called holy—the Son of God. [36] And behold, your relative Elizabeth in her old age has also conceived a son, and this is the sixth month with her who was called barren. [37] For nothing will be impossible with God." [38] And Mary said, "Behold, I am the servant of the Lord; let it be to me according to your word." And the angel departed from her.

MARY VISITS ELIZABETH

[39] In those days Mary arose and went with haste into the hill country, to a town in Judah, [40] and she entered the house of Zechariah and greeted Elizabeth. [41] And when Elizabeth heard the greeting of Mary, the baby leaped in her womb. And Elizabeth was filled with the Holy Spirit, [42] and she exclaimed with a loud cry, "Blessed are you among women, and blessed is the fruit of your womb! [43] And why is this granted to me that the mother of my Lord should come to me? [44] For behold, when the sound of your greeting came to my ears, the baby in my womb leaped for joy. [45] And blessed is she who believed that there would be a fulfillment of what was spoken to her from the Lord."

MARY'S SONG OF PRAISE: THE MAGNIFICAT

[46] And Mary said,
"My soul magnifies the Lord,

[47] and my spirit rejoices in God my Savior,
[48] for he has looked on the humble estate of his servant.
For behold, from now on all generations will call me blessed;
[49] for he who is mighty has done great things for me,
and holy is his name.
[50] And his mercy is for those who fear him
from generation to generation.
[51] He has shown strength with his arm;
he has scattered the proud in the thoughts of their hearts;
[52] he has brought down the mighty from their thrones
and exalted those of humble estate;
[53] he has filled the hungry with good things,
and the rich he has sent away empty.
[54] He has helped his servant Israel,
in remembrance of his mercy,
[55] as he spoke to our fathers,
to Abraham and to his offspring forever."
[56] And Mary remained with her about three months and returned to her home.

THE BIRTH OF JOHN THE BAPTIST

[57] Now the time came for Elizabeth to give birth, and she bore a son. [58] And her neighbors and relatives heard that the Lord had shown great mercy to her, and they rejoiced with her. [59] And on the eighth day they came to circumcise the child. And they would have called him Zechariah after his father, [60] but his mother answered, "No; he shall be called John." [61] And they said to her, "None of your relatives is called by this name." [62] And they made signs to his father, inquiring what he wanted him to be called. [63] And he asked for a writing tablet and wrote, "His name is John." And they all wondered. [64] And immediately his mouth was opened and his tongue loosed, and he spoke, blessing God. [65] And fear came on all their neighbors. And all these things were talked about through all the hill country of Judea, [66] and all who heard them laid them up in their hearts, saying, "What then will this child be?" For the hand of the Lord was with him.

ZECHARIAH'S PROPHECY

[67] And his father Zechariah was filled with the Holy Spirit and prophesied, saying,
[68] "Blessed be the Lord God of Israel,
for he has visited and redeemed his people
[69] and has raised up a horn of salvation for us
in the house of his servant David,
[70] as he spoke by the mouth of his holy prophets from of old,
[71] that we should be saved from our enemies
and from the hand of all who hate us;
[72] to show the mercy promised to our fathers
and to remember his holy covenant,
[73] the oath that he swore to our father Abraham, to grant us
[74] that we, being delivered from the hand of our enemies, might serve him without fear,
[75] in holiness and righteousness before him all our days.
[76] And you, child, will be called the prophet of the Most High;
for you will go before the Lord to prepare his ways,
[77] to give knowledge of salvation to his people
in the forgiveness of their sins,
[78] because of the tender mercy of our God,
whereby the sunrise shall visit us from on high
[79] to give light to those who sit in darkness and in the shadow of death,
to guide our feet into the way of peace."
[80] And the child grew and became strong in spirit, and he was in the wilderness until the day of his public appearance to Israel.

INTRODUCTION

HOW TO USE THIS STUDY

Many of the letters and emails we receive at *Revive Our Hearts* are from women facing disappointment. Women dealing with the disappointment of:

- Being single much longer than they hoped.
- Being in a marriage with a man who isn't following the Lord.
- Waiting to have children.
- Parenting a young child who is difficult.
- Having an adult child who is not walking with the Lord.
- Waiting for a fulfilling career.
- Facing a discouraging medical diagnosis.

The list of potential disappointments is long. You likely have disappointments of your own. The question is, how do you deal with disappointment with grace? How do you continue to trust the Lord when your longings remain unfulfilled?

Luke 1 delivers the profile of a woman who knew what it was like to face disappointment. Elizabeth went on to become the mother of John the Baptist, but not until she'd already endured decades of infertility. Her story has much to teach us about God's grace in the face of our own disappointments.

As we look at Elizabeth's story, we'll also examine the lives of her husband, Zechariah, and her relative, Mary, as well as some others found in Scripture who faced disappointment. You may relate to any or all of them. We look to their examples, asking the Lord to teach us truth that applies to our own individual lives.

TIPS FOR USING THIS STUDY

Throughout this study, ask yourself these questions:

- What does this passage teach me about the heart, ways, and character of God?
- How does this passage point to Jesus and the gospel?

- Is there an example for me to either follow or avoid? If so, how should I seek to change in response?

Each week of study is divided into four suggested daily lessons. You are free to work at your own pace, finishing a day of study at a time or completing the entire week in one sitting.

As you go through the study, you may find it beneficial to listen to the audio series "A Portrait of Elizabeth".

Remember, the Holy Spirit is our primary teacher as we seek to understand God's Word. Jesus Himself told us that the Holy Spirit is a gift, and a "Helper" able to "teach you all things and bring to your remembrance all that I have said to you" (John 14:26). Secondary tools that can help you better understand the Word of God (but aren't necessary to complete this study) include:

- An English dictionary to look up the basic meaning of words
- Various translations and paraphrases of the Bible
- A concordance
- A Bible dictionary
- Commentaries
- A study Bible
- Colored pens or pencils to write in your Bible

To help you get more from this study, we've also included group discussion questions at the end of this booklet. You can join the discussion with our group of friends through the Elizabeth podcast created to accompany this study.

A PRACTICAL EXAMPLE

Elizabeth's story, though short, provides great insight into how to cope with disappointment in a way that honors the Lord. Through years of infertility, Elizabeth handles her unmet longing for a child with continued trust and obedience to the Lord. Her life may not have turned out the way she planned, but God allowed her to play a critical part in the unfolding of His redemptive story.

Through the next six weeks, may you find practical ways to put God's Word into action. And may you surrender your own disappointments as an act of praise to Christ—who is worthy.

SCRIPTURE MEMORY

Spend time meditating on and memorizing the following verse this week:

the Lord is good to those who WAIT for Him,

TO THE SOUL WHO SEEKS HIM

LAMENTATIONS 3:25

Week 1

RIGHTEOUS BUT WAITING

Introduction

Somewhere in the world sits a very disappointed scientist. Imagine scrolling through miles of data, enduring day after day of the same old, same old, hearing the same facts taught for decades and then . . . Eureka! You discover something new!

So it was with the scientists who identified Xena, a tenth planet located 10 billion miles from earth, with a diameter comparable to half the width of the United States. Discovery of a new planet? That's big news! Except . . . it hasn't been. Few of us have heard of Xena (and even fewer know the planet's official name, 2003 UB313), despite the fact that the discovery was made and announced more than a decade ago.[1]

Perhaps we earthlings are too busy with our own orbits to pay much attention to a planet so small and so far away. Xena entered our collective consciousnesses to lackluster excitement and fanfare.

Maybe you've never had a cosmic discovery ignored but you know what it's like to face disappointment. We all do. How should we respond when those disappointments come?

In the book of Luke, we are introduced to Elizabeth, wife of Zechariah, mother of John the Baptist, and cousin to Jesus' mother Mary. Elizabeth's story is most frequently told as background noise to the nativity, an afterthought to the wonder of Christ's coming birth. Or perhaps we look at Elizabeth in the rearview mirror as we consider her bug-eating son, John the Baptist, and wonder, *What did that boy's momma think of his strange ways?*

But Elizabeth's story wasn't always filled with such excitement. Her faith was forged in the fire of disappointment, and she has much to teach us about facing our own setbacks with hope and grace.

Read Luke 1.

THE BOOK OF *LUKE*

AN OVERVIEW

AUTHOR

Luke was not an eyewitness of Jesus' ministry (Luke 1:2), but a member of the second generation of the early Church. Church history records that Luke was a Gentile, and Scripture tells us that he was a "beloved physician" (Col. 4:14). Luke traveled with Paul, followed the accounts of Jesus' life "closely" and set out to write "an orderly account" of "all that Jesus began to do and teach" (Luke 1:3; Acts 1:1).

Both the Gospel of Luke and Luke's second book, Acts, were written for Theophilus. Scripture doesn't tell us who Theophilus was except for Luke's description of him as "most excellent." Though the letter was likely written to this specific individual, it has important applications for all believers (2 Tim. 3:16–17).

Day 1: SERVING AND SUFFERING

Though every word about Elizabeth in Scripture is contained in a single chapter, her story reveals many rich insights that can help us in our own walk with God.

Verses 5 gives us the setting for her life: "In the days of Herod, king of Judea, there was a priest named Zechariah, of the division of Abijah. And he had a wife from the daughters of Aaron, and her name was Elizabeth."

Let's stop and dig here for a moment. There's gold to be mined from these two sentences.

What was Elizabeth's husband's name? ______________________________

What was his vocation? ______________________________

The passage tells us that Zechariah was "of the division of Abijah." In 1 Chronicles 24:7–19, we learn that the Levites (priests) were organized into twenty-four divisions. Generally speaking, this rotation resulted in priests being summoned twice a year to serve in the temple in Jerusalem.

What does the passage reveal about Zechariah's heritage?

____

____

____

Look again. Whose family tree does this verse say Elizabeth came from?

____

____

According to Exodus 28:1, what was the role of Aaron and his family members?

____

____

Elizabeth was the daughter of a minister. She was married to a minister, and as her story unfolds, we'll see she became the mother of a minister.

Write out Luke 1:6 below.

____

____

____

How does this verse describe Elizabeth and her husband?

____

____

____

What high praise! If the characteristics of your own family could be recorded in Scripture, what words do you hope would be used? Record a few below.

____

____

____

____

____

Elizabeth comes from a family of faith. As long as there had been a temple, her grandparents had been serving the Lord in it. She married a man of faith, and together, they served the Lord and His people. They were a godly couple, in righteous standing before the Lord. They had a lifestyle of obedience.

And yet . . .

A faith-filled heritage, a godly marriage, and a righteous life did not insulate Elizabeth from disappointment. Verse 7 tells us, "But they had no child, because Elizabeth was barren, and both were advanced in years."

Look up Matthew 5:45. According to this passage, the sun rises on the ________ and the ________ and God sends rain on the ________ and the ________________.

In other words, we all receive blessings and disappointments. Elizabeth reminds us we can be righteous but waiting, serving the Lord and yet still suffering.

Look up each of the following passages. Draw a line to what each one teaches about waiting.

LAMENTATIONS 3:25	It is good to wait quietly for the Lord.
ISAIAH 40:31	We can have hope while we wait.
PSALM 37:7	Those who wait for the Lord will see their strength renewed.
PSALM 62:5	The Lord asks me to wait patiently for Him.
LAMENTATIONS 3:26	The Lord is good to those who wait.

Elizabeth waited for years and years and years to have a child of her own. We don't know her exact age, but we do know "both were advanced in years." On the surface, it must have seemed that empty arms were the only reward for Elizabeth's waiting.

Perhaps you know the exact brand of heartache Elizabeth did. You've longed for a child of your own for years, and your heart aches when you read of Zechariah and Elizabeth's unfulfilled longings. Or maybe you know a different kind of disappointment.

Replace the details of Elizabeth's disappointment with your own by filling in the blanks of the verse with details from your own life.

But ______________ (your name) had no ______________ (area of unfulfilled longing), because ______________________ and ______________________.

The Best Is Yet To Come

Are you ever tempted to believe that living a righteous life should exempt you from hurt or disappointment?

____

____

____

____

____

____

What promises do we have as followers of Christ who seek to live righteously? Look up the following passages and write the promise beside each one.

JOB 17:9 ____

____

____

PSALM 5:12 ____

____

____

PROVERBS 21:21 ____

____

____

Day 2: FAILING TO FRUIT

In Elizabeth's case, her womb was barren, but barrenness can take many forms. In agriculture, barrenness means "habitually failing to fruit."[2] It's an image of an apple tree with only leaves or seeds that refuse to send up sprouts. This is a picture of our own disappointments.

- Perhaps you've invested much in a relationship only to see it wither and die.
- Maybe you've poured countless hours into an idea or dream, but no growth ever comes.
- It may be that you've become disappointed in the ways your children have turned out. They used to be your little seedlings, but now their lives seem full of weeds.
- Maybe you've tried every treatment and remedy to cure an ailment, but they all habitually fail to produce lasting fruit.

List a few areas of your life where you feel discouraged while waiting to see the "fruit" of your investment.

____

____

While it's true there is much we don't know about Elizabeth, we don't see her giving up on obedience to God. We see a woman who is not serving God for His gifts but serving God just because He is good. She was commited to obey God, even when her longings were not fulfilled.

She was righteous but waiting *well.* Can the same be said of us?

Let's pause here for a moment. The disappointments you face today may feel major or minor. You may have wrestled with an unfulfilled longing for decades or just since you woke up this morning. In any case, know that God is paying attention. He listens to your longings. Take hope in this: Elizabeth's longings were not insignificant. They were the canvas God used to paint a magnificent masterpiece.

What truth does Psalm 56:8 reveal about God's response to our angst? ______________________

____

What does God ask us to do in 1 Peter 5:7? ______________________

____

Our worries, fears, longings, and deep sighs . . . God invites us to give them to Him. Why? Because He cares for us deeply.

In what area of life is obedience wearing you out? ______________________

____

What reward is promised to us in Galatians 6:9? ______________________

____

Consider how you can intentionally remind yourself of this Truth this week. Write your ideas below.

Day 3: THE LAND OF LONGING

The roots of our disappointments dig much deeper than our current situation or set back. To better understand Elizabeth's heartache and our own, let's pause and remember the first woman to ever experience disappointment.

Read Genesis 3. What disappointments did Eve face as a result of the Fall?

The seeds of many of our deepest longings were planted at the Fall. Sin forever fractured our relationships, warped our hearts, and strained our intimacy with the Father. The very soil beneath our feet is depleted by sin (Gen. 3:17).

You and I will always have unfulfilled longings this side of heaven. Living righteously doesn't mean we won't face disappointments. If we had all our longings fulfilled down here on earth, we wouldn't continue to long for a better place, our heart's ultimate home.

Theologian and preacher Charles Spurgeon is recorded as saying, "Anything is a blessing which makes us pray."

Is it your disappointments that remind you of your need for Jesus most often? Do your setbacks work like alarm clocks, reminding you to pray? If so, consider them a blessing.

During her years of infertility, how many hours must Elizabeth have spent in prayer? How often did this struggle drive her to her knees in desperation to see the Lord move? As we will soon see, none of it was wasted. The Lord was listening to Elizabeth. And He's listening to you, too.

Longings are not in and of themselves sinful. What is sinful is demanding that they be fulfilled now, or insisting on meeting those legitimate longings in illegitimate ways.

Reflecting on your own disappointments, how could Elizabeth have responded sinfully to her longing for a child?

How instead would you describe her response?

Who do you know that has faced disappointment with extraordinary grace? What can you learn from their example?

Say Psalm 27:14 out loud as a prayer, asking the Lord to help you wait on Him.

Day 4: HE IS WORTHY

Obedience to God is not a means of getting Him to do our will. We don't obey God so that He will make life easier for us. We obey God because He's God, He's sovereign, and He is worthy of our obedience.

Take some time today to reflect on who God is, using the passages below as your guide.

God, Colossians 1:17 tells me You are

God, Malachi 3:6 tells me You are

God, Psalm 33:6 tells me You are

God, Psalm 139:7–10 tells me You are

With these Scriptures in mind, write out a prayer to Him, telling Him you want to obey, even when you face disappointment.

SCRIPTURE MEMORY

Spend time meditating on and memorizing the following verse this week:

BUT I WILL HOPE continually & WILL PRAISE you yet more & more

PSALM 71:14

Week 2

THE BIGGER PICTURE

Introduction

We've all stood at the fork in the road—the juncture of hope and despair. It happens when we've been walking the same path for a very long time, long enough to wonder if our circumstances will ever change.

Maybe it's the road to physical healing . . .

Maybe it's the road to a restored relationship . . .

Maybe it's the road to financial freedom . . .

Or career success . . .

Or parenting victory . . .

Or deliverance from patterns of sin . . .

In Elizabeth's case, it was the road to motherhood. As she found herself "advanced in years" (Luke 1:7) and still barren, the road must have seemed impossibly long.

Some of us can be obedient and experience disappointment for a while, but then it gets into the long haul. We've obeyed and obeyed and obeyed God, and we've waited and waited and waited (and waited some more) to see Him move. We've walked with Him for years, but we're still not experiencing the answer to our prayers—the solutions to our problem, the change in the marriage, the change in that wayward child. Then it's easy to say, "I give up. This doesn't work." We look at the long road ahead, glancing back at the tear-filled miles we've already walked, and we end up on a detour toward doubt.

When faith in God's providence feels like a long road, we may come to the crossroads of hope and despair many times. Each intersection is an opportunity to renew our faith in God's promises and choose to take the next step of obedience.

WHAT IS THE GOSPEL?

In 1 Corinthians 15:1–4 Paul outlines the heartbeat of the gospel in three steps.

1. Christ died for our sins.
2. He was buried.
3. He was raised on the third day.

The gospel is this: Christ died for your sins so that you wouldn't have to. He paid the penalty for your sins. He was separated from His Father so that you and I never have to be. But He's no longer dead; we serve a risen Savior! These truths and all that flows from them will radically transform your life—and you will never be the same.

Write about a time when you found yourself at the juncture of hope and despair. Did you ultimately choose to trust in the Lord's care, or did you turn down the path of discouragement, defeat, and doubt?

Are you facing a situation currently that causes you to wonder if the Lord will come through for you?

Day 1: "WHO SINNED?"

Re-visit Luke 1:7. What other unfulfilled longings might have been connected to Elizabeth's unmet desire for a child? (Example: a family that looked like everyone else's.)

What's your best guess regarding how long they had waited to see God meet this desire?

Elizabeth and Zechariah faced their first wedding anniversary childless, surely hoping the year ahead would bring a child of their own. But then the next year passed, and the next, and the next, and still . . . there was no baby in their arms.

Surely, in their limited human perspective, the ship for this dream had sailed. Not only was their past disappointing as it relates to this longing to have children, but they were now at the place in life where there seemed to be no hope for their situation to ever change.

As if to rub salt in that gaping wound, in those days for a woman to be barren was seen as a sign of God's disfavor. People might have looked at her and assumed, *You must have done something wrong to cause God to judge you in this way.*

How do we know Elizabeth's barrenness was not a punishment from the Lord? (See Luke 1:6.)

Do you ever worry that your unfulfilled longings are a sign that God is displeased with you? Write about those fears below.

Look up Psalm 84:11.

What three promises do we find in this passage?

Read John 9:1–12. As you read, write down the questions that were asked by eyewitnesses to this miracle in the space below.

Q :

Q :

Q :

Q :

The miracle recorded in this passage happened within a generation of Elizabeth's pregnancy, and clearly the stigma of shame attached to unfulfilled longings remained. Surely, this man wanted to be healed. Perhaps he had spent many hours praying for the Lord to remove the burden of blindness, and yet until this encounter with Jesus, he still could not see.

What did the disciples assume blindness was a sign of (v. 2)?

Do we live in a culture that assumes disappointments are the result of personal sin? Explain your answer.

Jesus uses this encounter to teach a profound truth. Read verse 3 again. According to Jesus, did the blind man's own sin cause his affliction? ______________________________

Did his parent's sin cause their son to go blind? ______________________________

What alternate explanation does Jesus give for this man's suffering? ______________________________

This is important. Let's not race past it.

Certainly, there are times when suffering is the consequence of personal sin. Sometimes, suffering is simply an aftershock of the Fall, which placed a broken nature inside each of us. But there are times, like this man's blindness and Elizabeth's barrenness, when human suffering and disappointment shine a spotlight on something much more significant—the gospel.

According to verse 7, what is the meaning of "Siloam," the name of the pool where the blind man washed his eyes following his encounter with Jesus?

____

____

____

This blind man was *set free* to be *sent out* with a message about Jesus. If we fast forward just a few verses, we find him already preaching his first gospel sermon.

Read John 9:18–33.

How did the Jewish leaders react to the news that the blind man received his sight?

____

____

____

Write down his exact words, recorded in verse 25.

____

____

____

More than 1,500 years before John Newton penned the words to the famous hymn "Amazing Grace," this man was singing it. He couldn't answer all of the religious leaders' questions, but he could use his suffering to point toward Jesus.

Read verse 34. How did the leaders ultimately respond to this man's experience?

____

____

____

Though his most pressing desire (sight) had been met, other aches remained. He continued to wear a stigma (sinner) and a status (outcast). He had borne these labels his whole life, but now there was purpose behind them because they pointed others to Jesus.

Day 2: DAILY PRESENCE

Revisit Luke 1:8.

What was Zechariah doing in this verse?

____

____

____

The priests worked in rotations and were generally called to serve in the temple for a period of one week, twice a year.

According to verse 9, how was Zechariah chosen to go into the temple and burn incense?

____

____

____

It could seem to be just chance that Zechariah's division was chosen at this moment in history and that he drew the lot to burn incense. Some priests never got the high honor Zechariah received that day. Looking back, we can see that it wasn't chance; it was the act of a sovereign God who is orchestrating every circumstance in this universe and in our lives (including today's disappointments) to bring about His purposes.

Read Luke 1:8–17. Because of God's providence, what did Zechariah experience in the temple that day?

____

____

____

Look up the following verses. What does each one teach about God's providence?

PSALM 103:19 ______________________________

____

PROVERBS 16:9, 33 ______________________________

____

PSALM 145:15–16 ______________________________

____

Though serving in the temple was certainly a sacred task, Zechariah was simply doing what God called him to do, carrying out his responsibilities as a priest; and in the course of fulfilling his duty, God met him.

What happened in Luke 1:11?

As you obey God in what He has given you to do today, He will meet with you, too.

List the responsibilities on your plate today, even those that seem mundane or insignificant (laundry, dishes, dinner, work tasks, etc.).

Pray through Psalm 34:4–8, asking the Lord to meet you as you go through the day.

Day 3: SERVE WHILE YOU WAIT

What was Elizabeth likely doing as Zechariah was serving in the temple?

This was long before information spread with the click of a button. There was no way for Elizabeth to know what was happening with her husband. She didn't get to witness the angel of the Lord visiting Zechariah—this first indication that the Lord had heard their prayers and was about to answer them.

Right now, there are ways God is working in your life that you cannot see.

According to Job 26:14, what portion of the Lord's works are we able to see?

What hope does this give you as you think about areas of discouragement or disappointment where you are waiting to see God move?

Read Luke 1:41–45.

What truths did Elizabeth declare about Jesus even before His birth?

How could she have known these things?

Though the child growing in her womb was certainly cause for celebration, Elizabeth didn't allow herself or her child to be the focus. As a woman who had faithfully served the Lord all her life, she would have known that a Messiah was coming. She was attuned enough to the things of God to recognize when He was on the way.

As you face disappointments, how do you stay focused on knowing and serving the Lord? Write out your response below.

Day 4: A PICTURE OF THE TOMB

Elizabeth's longing for a child was eventually satisfied. Read Luke 1:57–66.

What did the arrival of this child make the people wonder about (v. 66)?

The circumstances surrounding John's birth were so remarkable that onlookers quickly moved past surface observations and wondered, "What then will this child be?"

The answer unfolds in Luke 3. He would be a mouthpiece for the message of Christ. Because his parents waited for him for so long and served the Lord so faithfully, when John spoke people were ready to listen. Elizabeth couldn't have known any of this during those long years when she waited for a child. But she did know that God was worthy of her continued devotion.

Beyond Luke 1, Elizabeth is never mentioned again in the Bible. What became of her? We don't know . . . and it doesn't matter. Her goal in life was to point people to God—for His purposes to be fulfilled. She had fulfilled her purpose by giving birth to a son, who was then given back to God. Her life reminds us that it's not about us; it's all about Him. This is the heart attitude of those that God has used throughout history to make Jesus known to our world.

I Wouldn't Choose It, But I Embrace It

All we can see is the immediate moment. We can't see the big picture. God had a picture He was painting; a tapestry He was weaving. This plan wasn't just for Elizabeth's life, her marriage, or her family but for the whole nation of Israel and beyond—for the whole world, not just in their day but in all of history. God has an incredible, great redemptive plan. His plan is to take fallen sinners and restore them to fellowship with Himself. He does that through His Son, Jesus.

Because of this, our disappointments illustrate the gospel. Like the tomb where Jesus' body laid for three long days before the resurrection, the hopes and dreams that feel dead and buried are simply waiting for the Lord to break through.

The disappointments you are facing aren't about you, any more than Elizabeth's barrenness was about her.

It's about Jesus.

Write down the apostle Paul's words found in Acts 20:24.

____

____

____

____

____

____

____

____

The NKJV translation records Paul's words this way, "But none of these things move me . . ."

In context, Paul was saying, "I'm going to experience persecution in every city I go. God has told me that." But he said, "None of these things move me; nor do I count my life dear to myself, so that I may finish my race with joy, and the ministry which I received from the Lord Jesus, to testify to the gospel of the grace of God" (NKJV).

What is Paul saying? "Persecution? I wouldn't choose it, but I embrace it. Why? Because all that matters to me is that the gospel is spread and God is pleased."

Unfulfilled Longings Are Gospel Opportunities

Everything that comes into our lives in one way or another, if we're children of God, is part of God's plan to make Jesus known to the world. If only we could see that! If only when we can't see it, we could trust it. God had a plan, a purpose, for Elizabeth's life. She was a little, itsy-bitsy part of a much bigger picture.

Are you willing to see your unfulfilled longings as an opportunity to display Christ? If so, declare it!

I wouldn't choose ___________________, but I embrace it, because my life is about proclaiming Christ.

When we make the choice to say "yes," we experience contentment, even in the face of deep disappointment. Contentment is not the same as being "zen" or denying that disappointments exist in our lives. It's coming to the crossroads of hope and despair and choosing hope, trusting that God is already working to redeem our suffering for His glory. This is the choice that moves us from set free to sent out in Jesus' name.

Like the blind man who received sight and Elizabeth who received her long-awaited son, choose to use your circumstances to point toward the Savior. There is no guarantee God will fulfill every desire this side of heaven, but it is possible to point to the Savior in every single season of disappointment.

Oh God, I know that you know what you are doing. I cannot explain it. I do not understand it. Though I wish, from my finite point of view, that it were different, deep in my heart I know that you do not make mistakes. Help me to use my dissapointments to reveal the gospel. Amen.

SCRIPTURE MEMORY

Spend time meditating on and memorizing the following verse this week:

REMEMBER THE FORMER THINGS OF OLD;
I AM God, and there is NO OTHER;
I am GOD, and there is none LIKE ME

ISAIAH 46:9

Week 3

THE BOTTOM LINE

Introduction

Most of us like to fix things.

We see a skinned knee; we bandage it.
The house is a mess; we clean it up.
Our children make a spill; we wipe it right up.
Our friend's hair is out of place; we brush it back for her.

Using the sliding scale below, rate how often you feel the responsibility to "fix" the circumstances around you.

NEVER				SOMETIMES				ALWAYS	
1	2	3	4	5	6	7	8	9	10

We're used to straightening and fixing, but Elizabeth's story reminds us that sometimes we need to get out of the way and let God fix the problems in someone's life.

Day 1: THE BOTTOM LINE

Do you ever find yourself wanting to intervene in the lives of your mate, children, or friends when God is at work?

- Perhaps you'd like to spare them from what they're going through.
- Maybe you desperately wish you could convince them to turn away from a pattern of sin.
- Maybe it's simply a habit that isn't good for them that you'd like to convince them to evaluate.

Elizabeth might have been tempted to intervene, too.

Revisit Luke 1:11–17.

5 WAYS TO PRAY FOR OTHERS

1. Pray for them to have wisdom (EPH. 1:18–20).

2. Pray that they would grasp God's love (EPH. 3:16–19).

3. Pray for them to grow in discernment (PHIL. 1:9–11).

4. Pray for them to persevere in their faith (JAMES 1:12).

5. Pray for them to share their faith (PHILEM. 1:6).

Write down the promises the angel delivered to Zechariah.

Circle the words below that describe Zechariah's response found in verse 18.

EXCITED

SKEPTICAL

HAPPY

ANXIOUS

UNSURE

UNBELIEVING

CONFIDENT

TIMID

EAGER

Zechariah was in the temple of the Lord, face to face with an angel, hearing the words he had longed to hear, and yet his default was to doubt.

Can you think of a time in your own life when God moved powerfully and yet you struggled to embrace or see His hand?

Maybe you see someone you love in the story of Zechariah. It's obvious God is at work, and yet they don't seem to see Him or respond to Him. Write down any examples that come to mind.

Fill in the blanks for Gabriel's response found in verse 19.

"And the angel answered him, '______ am _________. I _________ in the _____________ of _____________ and I was _________ to _________ to you and to _______ _________ this _______ ________."

Gabriel is essentially saying, "You know it doesn't really matter who you are! I'm Gabriel, and I stand in the presence of God. Period. That's really all you need to know. I was sent to speak to you and bring you these glad tidings."

Talk about the bottom line!

Zechariah's experiences and doubts didn't matter. God was on the move! God was ultimately sovereign over Elizabeth and Zechariah's barrenness, and God is ultimately sovereign in our own lives.

What do each of the following passages teach about the sovereignty of God?

PSALM 115:3 ______________________________

____

ISAIAH 45:7 ______________________________

____

DANIEL 4:35 ______________________________

____

Remember that Zechariah and Elizabeth were faithful in their commitment to the Lord, and yet Zechariah had a temporary lapse in trust and expressed doubt that God could come through on His promise. In the same way, our heads can know that God is sovereign and our hearts can still doubt that He has authority over the many challenges we face.

Write out a prayer to the Lord, expressing your gratitude He is in control and confessing areas of doubt or fear.

____

____

____

____

____

____

Day 2: LETTING GOD BE GOD

Read Luke 1:20–23.

What do you think the reunion between Elizabeth and Zechariah was like? Describe it below.

While Zechariah was serving in the temple, encountering an angel, learning that he was going to be a father, and being struck mute for his disobedience . . . picture Elizabeth. She is sitting at home, waiting for her husband to finish his priestly tour of duty.

After he's done his week of service, he comes back home. She likely knows nothing that's gone on. Her husband arrives back home, and he can't talk. She's got a different husband. Somehow he figures out how to explain to her that he has seen an angel, that God has appeared to him, and that she—who is past childbearing years—is going to have a son. Talk about important news!

While Zechariah certainly received joyous news, he also faced a new disappointment: He could no longer talk!

What are some ways Elizabeth could have tried to "fix" or control the situation?

Scripture doesn't record Elizabeth's exact response, but based on what we know about Elizabeth's character and the rest of her story, what is your educated guess about how Elizabeth responded to Zechariah's condition and his news?

We don't know what Elizabeth thought; we don't know what she said. But the appearance in this passage is that she let God be God—not only in her own life but in God's dealing with her husband.

Who do you know who is facing disappointment right now? How are you tempted to "fix" or take control of the situation?

There are things God will do or allow to happen in your husband's life, in the lives of your parents, in the lives of your children, in the lives of your siblings and others, that you know and love that you cannot understand or explain. That's where we have to go back to this basic principle that God is God, and we are not. We choose to trust that He will have His way in the lives of those we love.

Spend time carefully reading through Job 38–39.

Record Job's response to the Lord found in Job 40:4–5. Compare Job's words with the psalmist's found in Psalm 46:10.

JOB 40:4-5 ______________________________

____

____

____

____

____

PSALM 46:10 ______________________________

____

____

____

____

____

Zechariah was struck silent by an angel, but perhaps Elizabeth chose silence as an expression of her trust that God was in control in her and her husband's lives.

Write out any areas where you struggle to simply let God be God in your life or in the life of someone you love.

____

____

____

Take some time to simply sit quietly, perhaps while reading your Bible or listening to a favorite worship song. Surrender your impulses to fix or be in control to the Lord, asking Him to help you trust that He is God in every situation.

Day 3: A LEGACY OF "YES!"

When her husband returned mute from a business trip with the news they were going to be parents, Elizabeth had been walking in the commands and ordinance of God for a lifetime.

Who do you know who has walked with the Lord for decades? ______________________

What fruit do you see in his or her life? ______________________

A life of obedience to God when it's not as difficult is the best preparation for a life of obedience when the real challenges come. Don't think you can live your own way, and then when the big tests come, you'll suddenly have a heart to obey God. It doesn't work like that. Everyday obedience develops the muscles needed when the going gets tough.

Though the record of Elizabeth's life is short, it is loaded with yeses. Next to each verse, write what Elizabeth said "yes" to.

LUKE 1:5 ______________________

____

LUKE 1:6 ______________________

____

LUKE 1:24 ______________________

____

LUKE 1:40-44 ______________________

____

LUKE 1:45 ______________________

____

LUKE 1:56 ______________________

____

LUKE 1:60-61 ______________________

____

Whether it was marrying a priest, embracing geriatric motherhood, or choosing the name of her child, Elizabeth made a habit of saying "yes" to the Lord. In so doing, she created a legacy for her son, John, to follow.

Read the following passages, then record your answer for these two questions. What did John say "yes" to? What disappointments did he likely face as a result?

MATTHEW 3:1-6

MATTHEW 11:1-6

MARK 6:17-20

Because Elizabeth said "yes" to God, even in the face of disappointment, she taught her son to do the same. Even when it meant imprisonment and execution, John was obedient to the Lord, living out his parents' legacy of steadfast devotion to the Lord.

Consider your own response to disappointment. What message are you sending about who God is with your actions and reactions when life is hard and obedience is costly?

Write out Psalm 86:11 as a prayer, asking the Lord to teach you to obey Him daily so that you can pass on a legacy of "yes"!

Day 4: A CHANNEL OF BLESSING

Read Luke 1:26–56.

As Elizabeth's story continues to unfold, we find that in the sixth month of her pregnancy, the same angel who visited Zechariah visits a virgin named Mary. It seems dramatic birth announcements are Gabriel's specialty, because this time he delivers the news that Mary will be the mother of the Christ Child.

According to Luke 1:36, what is the relationship between Elizabeth and Mary?

____

____

We can assume that Mary and Elizabeth were close, because almost as soon as Mary hears the news about her baby, she races to tell Elizabeth.

How long did she stay in Elizabeth's home (v. 56)? ______________________________

How many months did Elizabeth keep her pregnancy hidden (v. 24)? ______________________________

What month did Gabriel appear to Mary (v. 26)? ______________________________

Let's do the math. Elizabeth was six months pregnant when Mary arrived, newly carrying the Savior in her womb. Mary stayed for three months, meaning she packed her bags and headed home right about the time Elizabeth's son arrived, or perhaps she stayed for John's birth.

Two women:

- One old, one young.
- One married, one engaged.
- One in the final trimester of pregnancy, one just beginning to experience morning sickness.

And yet both women experienced both disappointment and the unmerited favor of the Lord.

What do you think Elizabeth and Mary talked about during their three months together?

____

____

____

____

Elizabeth's faithfulness to the Lord, regardless of circumstances, left an unquestionable mark on her husband, her son, and on Mary. God used Elizabeth to encourage Mary in her faith. Perhaps Mary needed some reassurance, someone who would believe what God said to her.

According to 2 Corinthians 1:3–5, what is one of the reasons Christ comforts us? (Keep this passage in mind. We will revisit it next week.)

___

___

___

___

As you face disappointments, you have a choice. You can face challenges kicking and screaming, questioning God's sovereignty and goodness, or you can let God be God and say "yes" to His work in your life. Both choices make an impact. When we choose to respond like Elizabeth, we become a channel of blessing to others around us.

Whose life has been an example to you of saying "Yes, Lord"? Consider writing them a letter, thanking them for their obedience and explaining their impact on your life.

SCRIPTURE MEMORY

Spend time meditating on and memorizing the following verse this week:

this HOPE will not DISAPPOINT us, because GOD'S love has been POURED OUT in our hearts through the HOLY SPIRIT who was GIVEN to us.

ROMANS 5:5 CSB

Week 4

HOPE FOR A DISAPPOINTED WORLD

Introduction

The stands were full. The cameras were rolling. The jockey was ready. But disappointment, not celebration, ultimately became the mood of the day.

Silver Charm was poised to win big. The American champion thoroughbred race horse was poised to seize the elusive Triple Crown, an award granted to only thirteen horses in the past 100 years.[3] He had already won the Kentucky Derby and the Preakness Stakes. He simply needed to cross the finish line first at the Belmont Stakes to go down in history as a Triple Crown winner, a champion among champions.
But it was not to be.

Silver Charm was bested by Touch Gold by less than a single stride. As the horse's rider, Gary Stevens, dismounted, he said, "If anyone ever had any doubt about how hard it is to win the Triple Crown . . ." before his voice trailed off and he said no more.[4] More than a decade later, we can still feel his disappointment. He was close enough to victory to taste it, and yet not close enough to take a bite.

If we think of disappointment like an infectious disease, hope is the antidote. Elizabeth teaches us how to hold on to true hope in the face of disappointment and how to be an ambassador of hope to a disappointed world.

How does the Bible Describe the World?

- **Full of trouble** (JOHN 16:33)
- **Temporary** (1 JOHN 2:17)
- **At war** (2 COR. 10:3)
- **Loved** (JOHN 3:16-17)

Write out Romans 5:5 below. What does this verse teach us about the source of our true hope?

____

____

____

____

____

____

____

Day 1: THE LONG ROAD OF HOPE

Scripture only records Elizabeth talking in three places. Record her exact words under each Scripture reference below.

Based on these few brief interactions, how would you describe Elizabeth's countenance? Circle all that apply.

UPBEAT
MELODRAMATIC
GRUMPY
CHEERFUL
STEADY
FUNNY
MATTER-OF-FACT
EMBITTERED
LOW-KEY
HIGH-MAINTENANCE
HAPPY
CRITICAL
FAITHFUL

Other than the moment when she announced her baby's name rather matter-of-factly (v. 60), the only times we see Elizabeth speak she's talking about God.

And did you notice? In every single situation she was waiting.

As she waited to give birth to her much-anticipated child, she declared, "Thus the Lord has done for me in the days when he looked on me, to take away my reproach among people" (v. 25).

As she waited to see her Savior face to face, she said, "And why is this granted to me that the mother of my Lord should come to me?" (v. 43).

And as she waited for her husband to once again be able to speak for himself, she spoke on his behalf: "No; he shall be called John" (v. 60). Even in the declaration of her child's name, she was being obedient to God, agreeing to give him the name the angel had spoken to her husband.

These are not the words of an embittered woman, though she had faced the disappointment of infertility for decades.

These are not the words of an angry woman, though her husband had been struck mute as a result of his unbelief.

These are not the words of a weak woman. She listened to the Lord and obeyed, despite the murmurings of the crowd.

These are the words of a woman anchored by *hope.*

Define the word hope in the space provided.

____

____

____

____

Think of hope like a pearl produced within a clam's shell. In order for the pearl to develop, an irritant must be present. Natural pearls form when a foreign object such as sand, grit, or a parasite work their way past the clam's hard outer defense. As a means to protect itself, the clam coats the irritant in layers of fluid until a beautiful pearl is formed.

So it is with hope.

We have every reason to think that Elizabeth held on to the hope that God would come through in every heartache. Will we follow her example and hold on to hope as we face disappointments of our own?

In Romans 5, Paul encourages believers to "rejoice in hope of the glory of God" (v. 2). But he doesn't stop there. According to verse 3, what does Paul ask us to rejoice in? ______________________

Paul goes on to describe a progression in verses 3–5. Record it by filling in the blanks below.

Suffering produces ➡ ____________ produces ➡ ____________ produces ➡ ____________.

Elizabeth was a woman of character, but that character didn't just happen. It was forged in the fire of disappointment. Her years of longing to see the Lord work taught her how to hope.

Can you look back at your own life and identify any disappointments that taught you to find your hope in the Lord? Write about them below.

Day 2: YOUR KINGDOM COME

Does Scripture tell us that Elizabeth and Zechariah prayed about her disappointments? (Hint: Review Luke 1:13.)

We don't know how long they had prayed, but it appears that it was probably many years. They'd cried out to God, "Lord, bless us with a child."

We know the end of the story, but Elizabeth had no way of knowing how things would turn out. Isn't that the way it is when we have unfulfilled longings? We pray about it. We obey God to the best of our ability, the best we know how to do, and we're stuck in this immediate situation with disappointment or pain.

Elizabeth and Zechariah had years of prayers, planted and watered with tears. Lots of tears. And yet for a long time, there was no growth. As we pray for the Lord to hear our prayers for prolonged seasons, how can we continue to hope for His answer?

In Matthew 6:9–13, Jesus gives us a model for how to pray. Write out this familiar prayer in the space provided below.

Next to verses 9–10, write out this part of Jesus' prayer in your own words.

Matthew 6:9-10	
[9] Pray then like this: "Our Father in heaven, hallowed be your name. [10] Your kingdom come, your will be done, on earth as it is in heaven.	

Before we pray for anything else, no matter how urgent, no matter what kind of crisis we may be in, Jesus taught us to pray that God's name will be glorified. His name represents all that He is. We want to pray that God's kingdom will come and His will be done.

As we pray about areas of disappointment and longing, Jesus encourages us to do so in the context of wanting God to be glorified, as His reign and rule is exerted and asserted in this world. It's wanting the will of God to be done.

- Why are you praying for the salvation of your lost husband?
- Why are you praying for the healing of your marriage?
- Why are you praying for that person who's just been given a terminal diagnosis?
- Why are you asking God to give you a mate?
- Why are you asking God to give you a child?
- Why are you asking God for financial provision?

Like Elizabeth and Zechariah's prayer for a child, these are appropriate things to take before the Lord as petitions. But the question is *why?* What's our priority, and what matters to us? Are we driven to pray for those things because of a love for God's name, glory, kingdom, and will, or are we asking for our personal well-being and satisfaction and happiness? It's a matter of priority and order.

Go back to the list of disappointments you recorded in week 1. Evaluate each disappointment, asking yourself, *Is my goal God's glory or my comfort in this situation?*

God did answer Elizabeth's prayer for a child with a "yes," but more importantly, He responded to her desire to use her life to glorify *His name.*

In hindsight, we can see what Elizabeth must have already known: Her story was not about her. God used all those years of disappointment and waiting. He used Elizabeth's example of walking "blamelessly in all the commandments of the Lord" (Luke 1:6). He used her husband's unbelief. He used it all to write a miraculous story about His power and glory.

He desires to do the same in our lives.

Look up Romans 2:24.

According to Romans 1:7, who did Paul write these words to? ______________________________

Paul was writing to followers of Christ in this verse, reporting the tragic news that God's name was being twisted because of them. Whew! To what extent are we, as believers, responsible for the world having a poor view of God because we don't hallow His name and desire His glory over our own comfort?

In contrast, what impression did others have as a result of Elizabeth's faith? (See Luke 1:66.)

____

____

____

Write out a prayer below, asking the Lord to help you seek His glory in the face of disappointment.

____

____

____

____

Day 3: PRAYING IN HOPE

When the disappointments keep coming, why should we keep praying? Scripture answers that question with the beautiful promises of God. Today's lesson is Scripture heavy. Take the time to read through these passages slowly, intentionally focusing on the promise God delivers in each one.

Hope For Our Health Disappointments

Isaiah 41:10
Philippians 3:20–21
James 5:14

Hope For Relational Disappointments

John 16:33
Psalm 34:18
Revelation 21:4

Hope For Spiritual Disappointments

1 John 1:9
Jeremiah 31:3
1 Peter 5:6–7

Hope To Keep Praying

James 1:5–6
Romans 12:12
1 Thessalonians 5:16–18
Luke 18:1–8

Day 4: AMBASSADORS OF HOPE

Disappointment entered the world long before Elizabeth had to face her unmet longings for a child, and it exists among us long after her story was recorded in the book of Luke.

Read Genesis 3:1–8.

Was Eve motivated to sin by an unfulfilled longing? If so, what was it?

____

____

____

When Eve took the first bite of that fruit, I really believe she didn't stop to think about the consequences—the consequences in her own life, the consequences in her marriage, the consequences in her children and her grandchildren and her great-grandchildren and her great-great-grandchildren and in women and men and marriage and culture and history and all of life forever. She didn't stop to think and count the cost. A cost that, among other things, would mean living in a disappointing world.

Look at the curse handed down by God in Genesis 3:14–19.

What disappointments was the serpent forced to face as a result of the Fall?

____

____

What disappointments was Eve forced to face as a result of the Fall?

____

____

What disappointments was Adam forced to face as a result of the Fall?

____

____

According to Romans 5:12, what primary consequence entered the world as a result of sin?

____

____

Adam and Eve's sin took God's perfect creation and broke it to its core. Our hearts are broken, plagued by sin. Our relationships are broken, infected with pride and selfishness. Our planet is broken, groaning under the weight of sin and death. And as a result, each of us must deal with the deep longing for redemption.

We live in a culture in desperate need of true hope. So did Elizabeth. She was part of a Jewish culture who had been looking for a savior for generations.

Revisit Elizabeth's words recorded in Luke 1:41–45.

Elizabeth was the first person to declare Jesus as the long-awaited Savior. Mary agreed to obey the Lord, but Elizabeth was the first to say that Jesus was Lord. In so doing, Elizabeth became the first ambassador of hope.

We can follow Elizabeth's example by sharing the gospel and declaring hope to a disappointed world.

What word did Paul use to describe himself in Ephesians 6:20? ____________________________________

What does Scripture call each of us to be in 2 Corinthians 5:20? ____________________________________

How do we do that?

First Peter 3:15 gives us the answer. Write it out below.

____

____

____

____

____

____

As followers of Christ, we are ambassadors of hope. We know that Christ is sovereign over every unfulfilled longing and that He alone is able to redeem every disappointment caused by sin and brokenness. Fill in the statement below as a way of accepting Christ's commission to be ready to talk about the hope you have in Him.

My name is ________________, and I am an ambassador of hope.

SCRIPTURE MEMORY

Spend time meditating on and memorizing the following verse this week:

blessed

ARE THE PURE IN HEART,

for they shall

SEE God.

MATTHEW 5:8

Week 5

THE FINAL CHAPTER

Introduction

Imagine if every great story ended in a cliffhanger.

What if we were left to wonder if Cinderella's foot fit inside the glass slipper?

What if we didn't know for sure whether Little Red Riding Hood would escape the claws of the wolf or were left to guess if the bears discovered Goldilocks sleeping in Baby Bear's bed?

Stories without endings are a frustration, not a comfort to us. We want to know that everything is eventually set right and that the characters get their shot at "happily ever after."

At first glance, Elizabeth's story seems to end with a question mark. We're not told exactly how her life ends. However, Scripture doesn't leave us guessing. It is rich with promises, meant to reveal the last chapter for all who believe in Christ.

Day 1: THE FINAL CHAPTER

Read Luke 1:80. What does this passage reveal about the end of Elizabeth's story?

____

____

____

____

____

____

____

____

____

The End is the Beginning

The Bible ends with these powerful words:

He who testifies to these things says, "Surely, I am coming soon." Amen. Come, Lord Jesus!

The grace of the Lord Jesus be with all. Amen (Rev. 22:20–21).

And yet this is really just the beginning of the rest of the story. From the moment the Lord returns for us, He will usher in a new reality free of pain, sorrow, and death, and He will reign forever and ever.

We repeat John's words, "Come, Lord Jesus!"

It's okay if you couldn't think of much to write in response to the question above. When it comes to Elizabeth's story, the Bible leaves out the details we're dying to know.

- Did Elizabeth get to see her boy grow up?
- Did he remain an only child?
- How did Elizabeth and Zechariah die?
- Did they live long enough to see Jesus begin His earthly ministry?
- Were they proud of or embarrassed by their son's strange ways?
- We don't know, and yet Scripture is not as silent as it seems at first glance.

Write down how you hope Elizabeth's story ended.

____

____

____

____

____

____

____

One of the things I love about the Lord is that He always writes the final chapter, and He knows that final chapter long before we can ever see it ourselves.

Fill in the blanks for Isaiah 14:27 below.

For the ____________ of ____________ has ____________,

and who will ____________ it?

____________ ____________ is ____________ ____________,

and ____________ will ____________ it ____________?

Elizabeth may have written her story very differently. She likely would have chosen to have children much earlier in her life. Maybe she would have written the script to include lots of children. Perhaps she hoped her story would include a child more "normal" than John. And yet God wrote the story He had in mind for Elizabeth. He is writing the story He has in mind for you as well.

Elizabeth waited for years to become a mother. She faced barren month after barren month. And when all hope of the story she hoped for seemed lost, God intervened supernaturally, bringing an end to her disappointment in an extraordinary way.

God had a plan for Elizabeth. God has a plan for you.

Match each of the following references with the truth it teaches about God's plan.

EPHESIANS 2:10	For we are his workmanship, created in Christ Jesus for good works, which God prepared beforehand, that we should walk in them.
PROVERBS 19:21	Many are the plans in the mind of a man, but it is the purpose of the Lord that will stand.
JOB 42:2	And we know that for those who love God all things work together for good, for those who are called according to his purpose.
ROMANS 8:28	"I know that you can do all things, and that no purpose of yours can be thwarted."

Every day of Elizabeth's life, God was moving her toward the day when the Messiah would come; that's the context in which she and her husband lived. As Elizabeth faced the disappointment of infertility, God was busy preparing the way for the coming of Jesus. When God has a purpose in mind that He wants to fulfill, there is nothing that can stop Him.

As Elizabeth locked eyes with Jesus' mother, Mary, she knew the ending that mattered most. Her deepest longings would be met. Christ was on His way!

What promise does Christ give us in Revelation 22:12? ____________________

Like Elizabeth, we are waiting for the Messiah. He arrived once already as a baby, but that is not the end of the story. He will come again. How does Revelation 19:11–21 describe Christ's second coming? ____________________

When it comes to our disappointments, Christ has already written the ending. A day is coming when He will return for us. Just as Elizabeth's longings melted away with the news that Jesus would soon be born, we can hold on to the hope that, because of Jesus, our stories have a remarkable ending.

Write out a prayer thanking God that His plans can be trusted and that your hope is in the promise of His return.

____

____

____

Day 2: PROMISED JOY

Circle back to Luke 1:14.

What two emotions did the angel Gabriel promise Zechariah would experience?

How would you describe the difference between joy and gladness? Look up the following verses to help with your definitions.

JOY	GLADNESS
Psalm 16:11	Psalm 45:7
Psalm 68:3	Psalm 100:2
Galatians 5:22	Acts 2:28

While the difference between these two emotions may not be crystal clear, Scripture does indicate they are both a gift from the Lord and a right response to His goodness in our lives.

Elizabeth and Zechariah were promised a child who would be a source of joy and gladness. Regardless of what you may be experiencing in your workplace, neighborhood, community, church, home, or in your own heart, regardless of whatever circumstances God finds you in today, if you are a child of God, you have the promise that one day there will be joy and gladness.

Maybe you're in a prolonged season of disappointment and think, *It's been an awful long time, and I haven't seen the joy yet.*

There is a kind of joy you can experience, even in the midst of those circumstances, because your joy is attached to God who never changes (Mal. 3:6).

But there is another type of joy that is not yet fully experienced . . . joy in the future fulfillment of God's promises.

As you close today's study, spend time meditating on Revelation 21:1–6.

Day 3: WE SHALL OVERCOME

Would you describe Elizabeth as an overcomer? Explain your answer.

____

____

____

____

____

____

____

To be an overcomer implies that there is a struggle, a battle, or hard times. In those moments, often what keeps us going, provides motivation, and encourages us to take the next step is a promise, something to look forward to.

Perhaps you're enduring long days in a job you don't love. What keeps you going to work in the morning? It's the promise of a paycheck.

How about enduring a diet or exercise program? What keeps you going? It's a promise of losing weight, of being fit and healthy.

Perhaps you're investing years into parenting and you're not yet seeing fruit for all of your labor because you're in the midst of it right now. It's hard. It takes pressing on. What keeps you going on? It's the promise that by God's grace, one day your children will grow up and become responsible adults.

What motivated Zechariah and Elizabeth to keep praying for a child for so many years? The promise that God heard them and He would respond to their cries.

Promises provide motivation and fuel hope to keep us going.

Skim through the letters to the seven churches described in Revelation 1–3.

These seven churches were all facing difficult and challenging circumstances. The Church in our day is facing increasing difficulties. We cannot expect the world to be a friend of grace. Following Christ and standing for truth will come with a share of disappointments. The world will oppose Christ, just as it did for Elizabeth's son, John.

Yet the believers in the churches in Revelation were exhorted to be faithful in spite of being in challenging circumstances. Elizabeth stands through the ages as an example of what it looks like to remain faithful and, ultimately, to overcome. Despite disappointments and heartaches, setbacks and opposition, all believers are ultimately overcomers.

Look up the following passages. Next to the reference, write what each passage teaches about overcoming.

JOHN 1:5 ______________________________

____

JOHN 16:33 ______________________________

____

1 JOHN 5:4–5 ______________________________

____

REVELATION 12:10–11 ______________________________

____

Read Revelation 20:4.

What did the saints do? They overcame; they conquered; they prevailed. They came to life and reigned with Christ for a thousand years.

Elizabeth certainly could have lost hope in the middle of her story. As we face disappointments and unfulfilled longings, we face a temptation to lose hope as well. But we must keep reading to the end of the story, because that's what gets us through the intermediate chapters, which are often full of hardship and tears, travail and labor, and pain and suffering. Look to the end of the story, and let your heart be encouraged.

Day 4: A SHARED HAPPY ENDING

Compare and contrast Genesis 3:4–19 and Revelation 22:1–6. What similarities do you see? What differences?

____

____

____

____

____

____

____

Disappointment entered the world as a consequence of sin. As fallen people in a broken world, we will continue to experience it. And yet what happened in the Garden of Eden will not have the final word. The curse will be reversed, and our deepest longings will be fulfilled.

What does Revelation 22:4 promise us?

____

____

____

John MacArthur writes, "In heaven, since we will be free from sin, we will see God's glory unveiled in its fullness. That will be a more pleasing, spectacular sight than anything we have known or could ever imagine on earth. No mere earthly pleasure can even begin to measure up to the privilege and the ecstasy of an unhindered view of the divine glory."[5]

Fill in the blanks for Matthew 5:8.

"Blessed are the ________ in ________, for they shall _______ __________."

Would you describe Elizabeth as "pure in heart"? Why or why not?

____

____

____

____

Seeing God, being in His presence, knowing Him fully, even as we're fully known (1 Cor. 13:12) . . . this is the deepest longing of our souls.

Write out the psalmist's prayer found in Psalm 42:1–2.

____

____

____

____

____

The details of Elizabeth's life and the disappointments she faced faded away in the presence of her Lord. Our stories share the same happy ending. Every unfulfilled longing we face right now, every disappointment that is yet to come, will ultimately fade away when we see Him face to face.

You may be dealing with a prodigal child. You cry yourself to sleep at night begging God to turn their heart.

You may be living in a marriage that, if God does not intervene, is not going to make it.

You may be dealing with physical issues, medical diagnoses, or physical pain.

How can you endure? How can you remain faithful? How can you keep from throwing in the towel? *How can you overcome?*

You look ahead. You look beyond the now. You lift your eyes up and look to the promises being fulfilled. You keep your eyes on the finish line.

Rewrite Psalm 42:1–2 as a prayer in your own words in the space below.

SCRIPTURE MEMORY

Spend time meditating on and memorizing the following verse this week:

PSALM 96:1

Week 6

ELIZABETH'S SONG

Introduction

Robert Ingersoll was an infamous nineteenth century infidel and agnostic. When he died, the funeral notices included this statement: "There will be no singing."

Those who don't know Christ have very little to sing about and *nothing* to sing about when it comes to death. On the other hand, those who do know Christ have many reasons to burst into song.

Luke 1 is filled with singing. Elizabeth exclaimed her joy over Jesus with such enthusiasm, we can almost picture her singing her excitement. Mary was filled with the Holy Spirit as she sang "The Magnificat," a hymn of praise. Zechariah's prophecy reads like song lyrics. Perhaps he couldn't help but sing as he too was filled with the Spirit.

Christians ought to be singing people.

In Charles Spurgeon's sermon, "The Memorable Hymn," he speaks of the hymn that Jesus and the disciples sang as they left their Last Supper celebration in the Upper Room. It was a Passover observance, and Matthew's Gospel tells us that they sang a hymn as they went out to the Garden of Gethsemane before Jesus faced the cross.

In that sermon, Spurgeon talks about how the children of Israel sang hymns to praise the Lord and Jesus was following in what was the Passover tradition of singing hymns.

> Beloved, if I had said that Israel could so properly sing, what shall I say of those of us who are the Lord's spiritually redeemed? We have been emancipated from a slavery worse than that of Egypt. As the Scripture says, "With a high hand and an outstretched arm, has God delivered us."
>
> The blood of Jesus Christ, the Lamb of God's Passover, has been sprinkled on our hearts and consciences. By faith we keep the Passover, for we have been spared. We have been brought out of Egypt, and though our sins did once oppose us, they have all been drowned in the Red Sea of the atoning blood

Songs of Scripture

You can find 185 songs in the Bible.

80 percent of these are Psalms.

Psalms isn't the only songbook in the Bible.

Song of Solomon is a love song between a bride and groom. Lamentations is a set of five songs mourning the fall of Jerusalem.

Psalm 119 is the longest song in the Bible with 1,732 words.

The two shortest songs are only seven (Hebrew) words long. (You can find them in 2 Chronicles 5:13 and 20:21.) [6]

of Jesus. The depths have covered them. There is not one of them left. If the Jew could sing a great *hallel* [the Hebrew word for praise], our hallel ought to be more glowing still.

It's true. Christianity has always been a singing religion. In times of plenty and in times of suffering, Christians have sung to the Lord, and we still do. Consider:

- First century Christians who suffered for their faith. Many went to their death, fearlessly, and in many cases singing songs of praise (Heb. 11:36–40).
- Paul and Silas in prison and yet singing hymns to the Lord in the middle of the night (Acts 16:25–34).
- Paul encouraging New Testament believers to address each other through song as they faced systematic persecution (Eph. 5:19; Col. 3:16).

Singing was their means of saying, "We're not victims. By God's grace and power, we're victors. He has triumphed gloriously!"

Elizabeth's story shows us how to do more than simply endure disappointment. She shows us how to sing through it.

Day 1: ELIZABETH'S BACKUP SINGERS

What do the following passages teach us about each woman mentioned?

SARAI—GENESIS 11:30 ____________________

____

REBEKAH—GENESIS 25:21 ____________________

____

RACHEL—GENESIS 29:31 ____________________

____

MANOAH'S WIFE—JUDGES 13:2-3 ____________________

____

MICHAL—2 SAMUEL 6:23 ____________________

____

Often when we face disappointment, there is a temptation to believe we're the only one. We may look around us and assess that no one else has to deal with unfulfilled longings in the same way we do. And yet the truth is disappointment is part of the human condition.

Elizabeth came from a long line of faithful followers of the Lord. But we also find many women in her lineage who struggled with the exact same kind of disappointment she did. While they sing through the ages of the grief of waiting for a child, they also sing of the faithfulness of God in the midst of disappointment. As we listen to Elizabeth sing about her story in this final week, these women are her backup singers.

Who do you know in your own life who has endured similar disappointments as you?

___

___

___

Do their lives encourage or discourage you?

___

___

___

Read 1 Samuel 1:1.

This verse tells us that Elkanah was an Ephrathite, meaning he was from Ephrath (also known as Ephrathah).

According to Micah 5:2, what is another name for this city? ___

Elkanah was from Bethlehem!

Like Zechariah and Elizabeth, Elkanah and his wife Hannah were Jewish people.

Read 1 Samuel 1:3–7.

Can we assess if Elkanah and Hannah faithfully served the Lord from this passage?

___

___

Like Zechariah and Elizabeth, Elkanah comes from a family heritage of faith. Like Zechariah and Elizabeth, they served the Lord faithfully year after year. And like Zechariah and Elizabeth, this couple faced the disappointment of infertility.

Read Hannah's prayer for a child, recorded in 1 Samuel 1:9–18. What strikes you about Hannah in this passage?

___

___

Without any confirmation that her prayer for a child had been answered, what did Hannah do next? (See verse 19.)

After pouring her heart out before the Lord, Hannah chose to worship. Despite any physical evidence that her desperate prayers for a child had been heard, Hannah praised the Lord. Where Elizabeth chose obedience in the face of disappointment, Hannah chose the sacrifice of praise.

Record your favorite parts of Hannah's song found in 1 Samuel 2:1–10.

We're all barren in some way. We all have prayers we desperately want answered. The Bible gives us clear instructions for what to do while we wait.

Read Isaiah 54:1–5.

What does this passage encourage us to do in the midst of our barrenness? (See verse 1.)

Set aside time this week to sing to the Lord. Here are a few ideas to get you started:

- Create a new Spotify playlist of your favorite worship songs.
- Participate in a mid-week service at church and sing along with the congregation.
- Take a walk and sing a favorite hymn along with the birds.

Make the choice to sing to the Lord even in the midst of the disappointments you will surely face this week.

Day 2: THE SACRIFICE OF PRAISE

Scripture is the ultimate choirmaster, inspiring the people of God to *sing!* The Psalms are particularly full of invitations to sing. Write out the following calls to worship found in the Psalms.

PSALM 71:23 ______________________________

____

PSALM 95:1 ______________________________

____

PSALM 98:1-7 ______________________________

____

PSALM 105:2 ______________________________

____

PSALM 150:1-6 ______________________________

____

God's people aren't invited to sing because we are never disappointed, but rather because we have hope beyond any temporary setback. We sing in hope that there is something better coming soon.

We will always have unfulfilled longings this side of heaven. If we didn't, we'd be satisfied with what we have here on earth. We wouldn't continue to long for a better place, for our heart's ultimate home.

It's not sinful to want a child. It's not sinful to want to be married. It's not sinful to want a more fulfilling career. It's not sinful to desire a financial provision. These longings are not, in and of themselves, sinful. What is sinful is when we demand they be fulfilled now or default to a posture of bitterness in the face of disappointment.

The deepest longings of our hearts cannot be filled by any created person or thing, and that's why we must learn to accept unfulfilled longings—to learn to live with them and surrender them to God.

How did Hannah surrender her unfulfilled longing for a child to the Lord?

Based on what you know of Elizabeth's character, do you think she also surrendered her desire for a child to the Lord? What do you think that might have looked like practically for her?

As we surrender our needs to God, they become material for sacrifice, something we can offer up to God in worship. Then as we surrender those longings, we look to Him to meet the deepest needs of our hearts. We trust Him to move in His time and in His way for His eternal purposes and glory.

How does Hebrews 13:15 describe praise?

In the face of disappointment, praise can feel like a sacrifice. We are tempted to lose heart or demand our own way instead. And yet, once surrendered, disappointments work like tinder, fueling our devotion to the Lord.

Are you willing to surrender your longings with a sacrifice of praise to the Lord? If so, write out your own version of this prayer:

Lord, I offer these disappointments up to You. I am willing to trust You to move in Your way—the way that will bring You the greatest glory. In the meantime, I'm willing to keep walking by faith, to keep serving You, and to praise You, just because You are God. Amen.

Day 3: REASONS TO SING

Even in the face of disappointment, God has given His people many reasons to sing. Today's lesson is Scripture heavy, with many reminders of why God's people should praise Him. Take your time as you read through these passages; don't race through to finish this section.

God's creation was made to sing.

Psalm 19:1–14
Luke 19:35–40
Revelation 5:13

Singing is an act of obedience.

Psalm 96:1–6
Colossians 3:16
Ephesians 5:18–20

Singing gives us strength in trials.

Acts 16:16–25
James 1:2–4
1 Peter 1:6–7

Jesus sang.

Matthew 26:30
Mark 14:26
Hebrews 2:11–12

When we sing, we are rehearsing for eternity.

Revelation 4:8–11
Revelation 7:9–17
Revelation 15:3–4

The redeemed *always* have cause to sing, even when our hearts are heavy or our circumstances feel overwhelming. I made myself a list in the last few days of some of the causes I have to sing, regardless of what is going on around me:

- Jesus died for me.
- My sins are forgiven.
- I've been declared righteous.
- We who were His enemies are now called His friends.
- We are beloved children of God.
- We have been adopted into His family.
- We are accepted in the beloved.
- We have peace with God.
- We have eternal life.
- We are eternally secure.
- No one and nothing can ever snatch us out of the Father's hand.
- If God is for us, who can be against us?
- Jesus stands before the throne of God, forever interceding on our behalf.
- He has said, "I will never leave you; I will never forsake you."
- He is always working to protect and to provide to meet our needs, no matter what is going on.
- God is on His throne, no matter what I feel and no matter what others may be doing that seems to be controlling the circumstances around me.

Make a list of your own. Write down the many reasons you have to sing.

____

____

____

____

____

____

____

____

Day 4: SING TO EACH OTHER

Review all of Elizabeth's story found in Luke 1.

How did Elizabeth use her circumstances to encourage others?

Through His Word, God does more than call us to simply *endure* disappointment. We are to use our lives to give God glory and encourage one another.

How does Ephesians 5:18–21 encourage us to communicate with each other?

What communication strategies does Colossians 3:13–16 encourage among us?

Can you think of a time when listening to another believer sing or singing with other Christians in corporate worship strengthened you? Write about it below.

Elizabeth's story is a reminder that we can face disappointment with grace because of the hope we have in Christ. Our stories can be a continuation of her song as we remind each other to look beyond our unmet desires and toward the One who will ultimately satisfy every longing.

Our circumstances at the moment will not last forever. There's something greater. There is something that surpasses them, that outreaches our circumstances. Elizabeth was able to face her disappointment because she knew a day is coming when every king, every president, every prime minister, every dictator, every husband, every boss, every leader, every politician—*everybody* will bow before His majesty, and Jesus will reign forever and ever.

Now that's something to sing about!

Charles Spurgeon said it this way: "We are ordained to be the minstrels of the skies, so let us rehearse our everlasting anthem before we sing it in the halls of New Jerusalem."

That's what we do here. We practice; we prepare. Start singing that song now. Join with those who've gone before, with the Miriams, the Hannahs, the Deborahs, the Marys . . . the Elizabeths. Join with those around the world who are singing it now. Sing in unison with others who have been redeemed. Don't let the disappointments of this life be your anthem. Tell what He has done for your soul. Tell how He has rescued you, and let's join together now and for all eternity in singing the song of the redeemed.

SMALL GROUP DISCUSSION QUESTIONS

Week 1:

- As our study of Elizabeth gets underway, is it your heart's desire to surrender your own disappointments as an act of faith and praise to Christ—who is worthy? If it is, can you share what difference you hope it will make in your life?
- From reading Luke 1, what new insights did you gain from Elizabeth and Zechariah's life?
- As Christ followers who seek to live godly lives, what does the Bible promise to us in Job 17:9, Psalm 5:12, and Proverbs 21:21? What does the Bible not promise?
- Charles Spurgeon is recorded as saying, "Anything is a blessing which makes us pray." How have you seen this statement to be true in your own life?
- Describe illegitimate ways a woman might sinfully fulfill these longings:
    - A single woman hoping for marriage
    - A mother whose adult child has walked away from the faith
    - A wife married to a man who isn't following Christ
    - A lonely woman seeking friendships
    - An infertile woman desiring a family
    - An overwhelmed mom with a difficult child
- Pray as a group thanking God for the power of His Word. Express the ways you personally want to grow from the Elizabeth study.

Week 2:

- What specific ways can we encourage one another to choose the right path of obedience when standing at a crossroads of hope and despair?
- Do you find any parallels of how Jesus experienced rejection from the world just as the man born blind in John 9:1-41?
- Can you think of examples of how human suffering and disappointment point to Christ and shine a spotlight on the Gospel?
- While we wait for God's hand to move, what attitudes or actions should we avoid that put the focus on ourselves and our circumstances?
- Explain how the choice to say, "yes!" to unfulfilled longings, as a way to proclaim Christ leads to contentment (Day 4).
- If a woman's life goal is to point people to God and for His purposes to be fulfilled, how will that mindset direct her daily life?

Listen in as women discuss this study in the Women of the Bible podcast by *Revive Our Hearts*. Find it at ReviveOurHearts.com/Elizabeth.

SMALL GROUP DISCUSSION QUESTIONS

Week 3:

- Slip on Elizabeth's sandals. Describe the range of emotions you might be feeling after hearing the news you will finally have the baby you've longed for. How might Elizabeth need to trust God in this new season of life?
- At one time or another, we've all struggled with doubt. What was the result of Zechariah's doubt in verse 20? How does doubting God's promises and sovereignty negatively impact our relationship with Him?
- What did you learn about the sovereignty of God from Psalm 115:3, Isaiah 45:7, and Daniel 4:35 (Day 1)? How will our daily lives be affected when we live in the confidence that God is in control and we need not fear?
- What has this week's lesson taught you about surrendering your impulses to "fix" people and circumstances rather than letting God be God (Day 2)?
- Who do you know that has walked with the Lord for decades? How has their life been a positive example for you to follow?
- Huddle up to pray for the people you care about using the five prayer prompts on page 27. Ask God to help you stay out of the way while He works out His plan.

Week 4:

- What is a Christian's source of true hope? What other sources do women often turn to for hope?
- Has there been a time in your life when you were able to rejoice in suffering (Rom. 5:2-5)? What does it mean to you that our suffering has an ultimate purpose to produce endurance, character, and hope?
- What does the world teach us about handling disappointment? How is a worldly view different than a gospel view of disappointment?
- Can you think of other women in the Bible or in your church who persisted in prayer for months, years, or decades before receiving an answer from the Lord? How would you like to emulate them?
- Brainstorm ways the members of your group can be ambassadors of hope in their circles of influence—neighborhoods, schools, workplaces, places of recreation, etc. Say in unison, "We are ambassadors of hope!"
- Close your group time by praying the Lord's Prayer together.

SMALL GROUP DISCUSSION QUESTIONS

Week 5:

- Do you ever think about what it will be like to see God's face in heaven (Rev. 22:4)? How does the future of living forever with the Lord change your outlook on the here and now? How are we able to "see" God's face even now?
- Describe how you are comforted by knowing God has a plan and He is writing a remarkable ending to your life story. What assurance do you gain from Isaiah 14:27?
- In which area of your life would you like to see joy and gladness emerge? Did you experience a fresh jolt of joy and gladness as you meditated on Rev. 21:1-6? What stood out from those verses?
- Describe how Elizabeth was an overcomer. Do you think of yourself as an overcomer? Why or why not?
- Which one of the passages on overcoming encouraged you (Day 3)? Can you share how it applies to your life?
- Read Psalm 42:1-2 together aloud. What are ways God satisfies our soul's thirst for Him?

Week 6:

- Elizabeth shows us how to sing through life's disappointments. Do you have a go-to song or hymn that reminds you of God's faithfulness?
- What do Elizabeth's backup singers all have in common (Day 1)? Do you know other people who've dealt with a similar disappointment as you have? How have they encouraged or discouraged you?
- Read aloud Isaiah 54:1-5. You don't have to have a beautiful voice to sing to the Lord while waiting for your prayers to be answered. Did you sing to the Lord this week? What difference did it make in your heart or attitude?
- How do you react to this statement? "Longings are not, in and of themselves, sinful. What is sinful is when we demand they be fulfilled now, or default to a posture of bitterness in the face of disappointment." Has a sinful response to unfulfilled longings ever been true of you?
- Discuss how Hannah and Elizabeth surrendered their desires to the Lord. What have you learned about yielding your desires to God?
- A day is coming when every knee will bow and every tongue will confess that Jesus Christ is Lord! Let's celebrate what He's doing in our lives, and the hope of what's to come by (what else?) . . . singing "Creation Sings the Father's Song" or another favorite worship song that testifies to the glories of our God and King.

Listen in as women discuss this study in the Women of the Bible podcast by *Revive Our Hearts*. Find it at ReviveOurHearts.com/Elizabeth.